This Means War: Putting on the Whole Armor of God Devotional

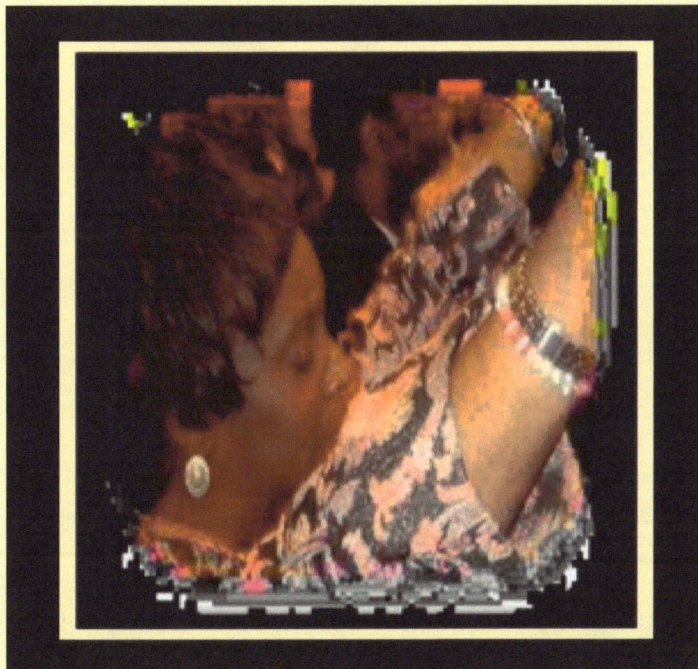

SDW [Spiritual Deliverance & Wholeness] Healing Ministries
Sistah's Of the Spirit S.O.S. &
The Mighty Men of Valor M.O.V.
Intercessory Prayer and Study Ministry
Reverend Sherrylyn D. Womble M.Div MSW

Founder

First Printing: 2017

ISBN 978-0-692-79181-3
90000

9 780692 791813

ISBN

SDW HEALING MINISTRIES PUBLISHING

3191 Rochambeau Avenue Suite #2C Bronx, NY 10467

For More Information on the Ministry:

Sistah's of The Spirit S.O.S. &
The Mighty Men of Valor M.O.V.
Reverend Sherrylyn D. Womble
Founder / Facilitator

Sistah's of The Spirit S.O.S & The Mighty Men of Valor M.O.V. Intercessory Prayer and Study Ministry. (Galatians 5:25, 2 Timothy 1:7) Our Intercessory Prayer -"I'll pray for you. You pray for me. Let's sit back and watch what God will do!"

Website: http://www.sosministries525.wix.com/sosministries

Facebook: @SOSSistahsoftheSpiritMinistries

Twitter: @SOSMinistry525

Instagram: sosministries525

You Tube: https://www.youtube.com/channel/UCWt2o6VCcowe82ba4hsGxEQ

Phone:(347) 589-7943 / FAX: (914) 930-4043
Email: sosministries525@gmail.com

Table of Contents

Expression of Gratitude

I thank God for the members of *Sistah's of the Spirit, the Mighty Men of Valor, Kingdom Aligned Prayer Line, and Ministry Moving International*. I would also like to thank my spiritual father and family, **Rev. Dr. John L. Scott,** and my St. John's Baptist Church family.

Rev. Sherrylyn Womble Founder and Facilitator
SDW Spiritual, Deliverance, Wholeness & Healing Ministries
Sistah's of The Spirit S.O.S. & The Mighty Men of Valor M.O.V.Ministries

Special thanks to my family, spiritual family, spiritual friends and supporters:

Deacon Sheila Alexander

Deacon Cynthia W. Brown

Brother Donnell Womble

The Late Rufus Gene Daniels

Deacon Julian Alexander

Brother Dominique Alexander

Brother Keats Alexander

Sister Lindsey Arrington

Brother Rodney E. W. Gibbs

Sister Salina Gibbs

Little Miss Layla Gibbs

Minister Cynthia Banks

Brother Gene Banks

Sister Crystal Turner-Moffatt

Deacon Delores Lee

Rev. Dr. Theresa Lloyd

Minister Lakisha Williams

Elder Lenore Artis

Pastor Shon Adkins

Apostle Kim Brewer-Insang

Mother Pearl Perry

Sister Satonia Hart

Sister Jessica Harris

Rev. Dr. Allen P. Weaver

Rev. Jeffrey Crenshaw

Mother Yvonne Turner

Minister Keith Johnson

Sister Beverly Zimmerman

Minister Danita Hammock

Minister Monique White

Minister Yvette Armstead

Pastor Annette Hayden

Rev. Dr. Zavette Smallwood

Elder Jaqueline Ferrell

Minister Patricia Wilson

Sister Sharon Hughes

Apostle William Hamilton

Sister Laurell Watson

Sister Yolanda Webster

OUR MISSION

The Mission of The SISTAH'S OF THE SPIRIT S.O.S. INTERCESSORY PRAYER AND STUDY MINISTRY is:

To Spread the Gospel of Jesus Christ and to grow spiritually by studying God's Word.

We believe in Praying in the Spirit. Declaring the Word of God over the lives of others and ourselves and watching God move.

We strive to be hearers and doers of His Word.

We walk in the Spirit and possess the Fruit of The Spirit (Galatians 5:22-23).

We diligently seek God's face and seek to bear good fruit. In all things we give God the Glory and work to uplift God's Kingdom.

We are available vessels for God's use. With Our Spirits, Hearts and Minds we utilize God's Anointing to aid in the healing, salvation and deliverance of others through intercessory prayer, praise and supplication.

We let our light shine in this sometimes dark world.

We strengthen ourselves daily through study and prayer and a fresh anointing of The Holy Spirit.

We strengthen and uplift others daily through:

Intercessory Prayer

Bible Study

Evangelism

And Outreach Ministry (Especially for Women)

THE MIGHTY MEN OF VALOR MINISTRY
OUR MISSION

"Our assignment is to develop Godly men within our Families, Churches, and The Kingdom of God; through prayer and studying the word of God." This is a new ministry under the umbrella of S.O.S. As the prayer line has developed we found the input and insight from men was invaluable to our growth as a ministry, as well as, to the growth of our anointed male counterparts. Judges 6:12 - And the angel of the LORD appeared unto him, and said unto him, The LORD [is] with thee, thou mighty man of valor. This ministry serves to strengthen men as intercessors and to strengthen their prayer life.

In closing The Sistah's of the Spirit - S.O.S. and Mighty Men of Valor Intercessory Prayer Ministries Motto is:

"I'LL PRAY FOR YOU. YOU PRAY FOR ME. LET'S SIT BACK AND WATCH WHAT GOD WILL DO!"

To God be the glory for the wonderful things He is doing for the ministry.

Mission

SDW [Spiritual Deliverance Wholeness] Healing Ministries
We are spiritually delivering wholeness and healing individuals and families through prayer and counseling. Our mission is to heal or enhance your mind, body, spirit, and lifestyle through life coaching. We provide Life Coaching for Families, Groups, and Individuals.

Preface

"Finally, my brethren, be strong in the Lord, and in the power of his might. Put on the whole armour of God, that ye may be able to stand against the wiles of the devil."
Ephesians 6:10-11 (KJV)

"For we wrestle not against flesh and blood, but against principalities, against powers, against the rulers of the darkness of this world, against spiritual wickedness in high places" Ephesians 6:12 (KJV)

For though we walk in the flesh, we do not war after the flesh: [4] (For the weapons of our warfare are not carnal, but mighty through God to the pulling down of strong holds; [5] Casting down imaginations, and every high thing that exalteth itself against the knowledge of God, and bringing into captivity every thought to the obedience of Christ" 2 Corinthians 10:3-5 (KJV)

"They are a nation without sense, there is no discernment in them. If only they were wise and would understand this and discern what their end will be! How could one man chase a thousand, or two put ten thousand to flight, unless their Rock had sold them, unless the LORD had given them up? For their rock is not like our Rock, as even our enemies concede." Deuteronomy 32:28-31 (NIV)

Introduction

Be Strong in the Lord! In order to conquer the enemy; in order to stand against the enemy's strategies; we must be strong in the Lord, draw strength from him and put on the armor the whole armor of God. The only way to draw strength from God is to read and study his Word and develop a trusting relationship with God.

"Strong" means physically powerful; capable of exerting great physical force; power might, and strength;

"Power" means force; unlimited power and dominion over everything

"Might" means strength, ability; great power of force.

"Wiles" means the deceits, craftiness, trickery, methods, and strategies which the devil uses to wage war against the believer. He will do everything he can to deceive and capture the believer. (Preacher's Outline and Sermon Bible – Commentary – The Preacher's Outline & Sermon Bible Galatians, Ephesians, Philippians, Colossians)

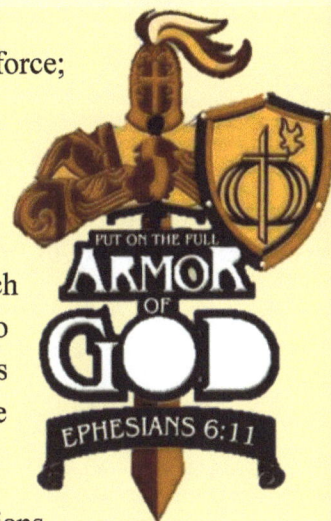

According to Word search, Preacher's Outline, and Sermon Bible – Ephesians Commentary,

"We can't put on the Armor of God or wage war against the enemy until our flesh is in subjection to God. We must be changed and strengthened on the inside first before it is shown on the outside. Others will see the change in your behavior and the way you live every day. Others will hear it when you talk; and others will feel the Holy Spirit when you walk in their presence. No amount of armor is worth the material it is made of unless the soldier has the heart to fight. We must put on every piece of armor, none of our flesh should be exposed or we could be wounded or spiritually killed. As believers and children of God we must walk in the power, might, and strength of God."

Who are you wrestling with?

I am on the battlefield for my Lord, I'm on the battlefield for my Lord; And I promised Him that I would serve him till I die. I am on the battlefield for my Lord.
When we accept the Lord Jesus Christ as our personal Savior, we become soldiers in God's army; we are enlisted in his army. The devil would make us think otherwise and want us to fight one another instead fighting him and his demons in prayer and spiritual warfare.

Principalities – "Demons that have oversight of nations and their responsibilities is spreading temptations and bondage; higher ranking and demonic authorities." Ephesians 1:21 (Preacher's Outline and Sermon Bible - Commentary – Ephesians).

Powers – "Demons that want to possess human beings, political kingdoms and symptoms." Colossians 2:15 (Preacher's Outline and Sermon Bible – Commentary- Ephesians).

Rulers of the Darkness – "Demons in charge of Satan's earthly business; territories." Colossians 2:15, Luke 22:53 (Preacher's Outline and Sermon Bible - Commentary – Ephesians).

Spiritual Wickedness in High Places – "Demons in charge of religion" (Preacher's Outline and Sermon Bible – Commentary – Ephesians)

This Means War!

We must understand how serious this Spiritual warfare is and what God is calling us to do. We need to surrender our all to God and study the word of God so we will understand the strategies of the enemy and what we need to do. We need to pray and seek God to see what part we play. I don't know about you but I am tired of allowing the enemy to do what he wants to do, say what he wants to say and sit back and watch him wreak havoc in the lives of the people of this world. We are to fight the enemy at all costs on every front. We are to fight the good fight of faith.

We must stop fighting one another and fight the true enemy through prayer and the word; through praise and worship; through dancing and singing. You may be on the praise team, in the choir, in the praise dance ministry; you may be the worship leader, the musician, choir director, or part of the five-fold ministry; or you may be an intercessor, watchman, gatekeeper or just a Child of God. We must equip ourselves to fight the enemy. We must ask God to show us who we truly are in the Kingdom.

We were called to destroy the enemy and prepare the people to worship and receive the Word of God. Some of us were called to preach the gospel. We can't pull down every stronghold, cast down every imagination and bring into captivity every thought to the obedience of Christ until we allow the Holy Spirit to take complete control of our mind, body, spirit, and soul. We can only wage war against the devil and fight the good fight of faith, if we persistently pray. As we continue in prayer, God will reveal and destroy every false idea we have about God, all the false doctrine and false teaching we have been taught. God will destroy it all. All self-righteousness will be destroyed.

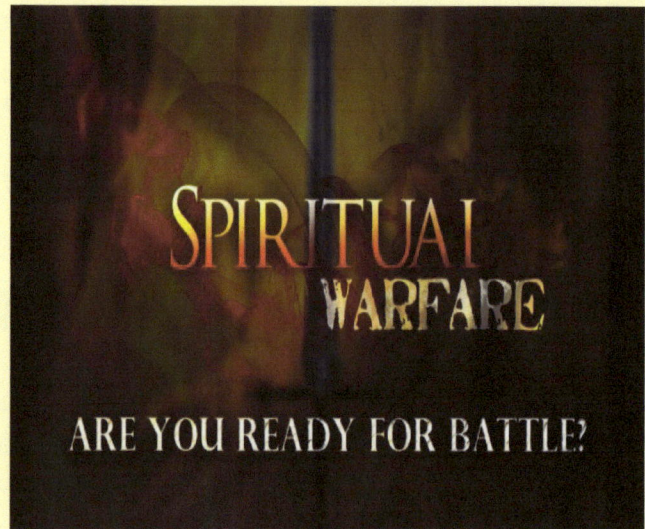

God did not create us to be alone but to be in fellowship and communion with him and one another. The first church followed these principles and thousands were saved. The resurrection of Jesus Christ was and is important; reading, studying, and mediating on the Word of God was and is important; spreading the Gospel of Jesus Christ was and is important. Jesus died and rose so we could walk in fellowship and communion with God. It is time for the dry bones to resurrect and the army of the Lord to move forward and upward. This means war! The enemy is seeking who he can devour (1 Peter 5:8). He wants to destroy our relationship with God, our families, and with one another. It is time for us to put him in his place.

There are some things that we must do to fight this war. First, we must enlist into the army of the Lord by accepting Jesus Christ as our personal Savior. We must surrender our mind, body, spirit, and soul and allow God to use us for his glory. We must realize whose we are and who we are. We must discern and recognize the call on our life and the ministry God calls us to serve in. We must study the Word of God daily and have a prayer life individually and collectively. God did not call us to just to be part of the five-fold ministry or a member of the praise team, the choir, and the praise dance ministry, worship leader, musician, choir director, intercessor, watchman, gatekeeper or just a Child of God. We have been strategically placed where we can destroy the enemy.

We Can't Do It Without God!

We can't live, move, or have our being without the Lord (Acts 17:28). It is the Lord that gives us strength to do anything, especially to fight the enemy. It is God who gives us strength to defeat the enemy. God is our rock and our salvation (Psalm 18:2; 62:6-7). God is a present help in the time of storm (Psalm 46:1). God will never leave us nor forsake (Deuteronomy 31:6, Hebrew13:5). In Deuteronomy 32:30-31, "the children of Israel lacked discernment, the ability to decide between truth and error, right and wrong, ability to think biblically about all areas of life. The children of Israel failed to discern the presence and power of God" (Preacher's Outline and Sermon Bible - Commentary - The Preacher's Outline & Sermon Bible – Deuteronomy) when they entered the Promise Land. They were more concerned about the enemies they would encounter than God's ability to empower them to defeat those same enemies. When God empowered them, one Israelite would chase a thousand and two would put ten-thousand to flight.

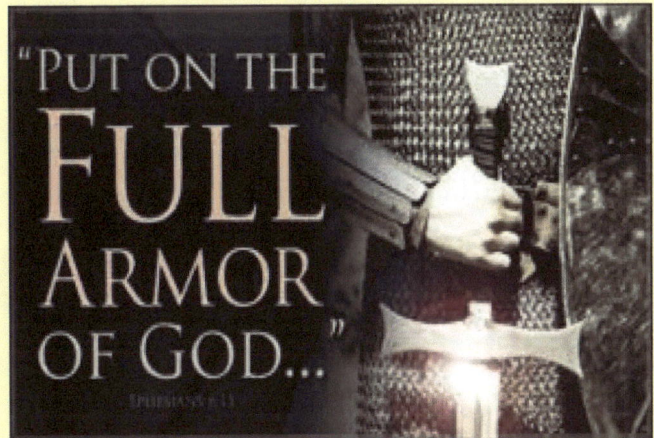

This is also true for us as Children of God. Our promised land is Heaven; this is the place where Jesus went to prepare for us while he sent the comforter to be by our side. We have and will encounter many enemies that are trying to destroy us day after day. The enemy wants to distract us and keep us from entering Heaven. There is victory in Jesus Christ and we cannot do it by ourselves or on our own. We must put on the full armor of God and allow God to use us. We have victory in Jesus Christ.

Father God, in the name of Jesus, I trust you and surrender my mind, body, spirit, and soul to you. Create in me a clean heart and a right spirit to serve you. Make me over and strengthen me. I will put on the whole armor of God daily. I decree and declare that you will grant me, according to your riches and your glory, strength and might by your Spirit in my inner man (Ephes. 3:16).
I decree and declare that you are able to do exceeding abundantly above all that I ask or think, according to the power that worketh in me (Ephes. 3:20). I decree and declare that you will strengthen me with all might, according to your glorious power, unto all patience and longsuffering with joyfulness (Col. 1:11). I decree and declare that you have not given me the spirit of fear; but of power, and of love, and of a sound mind. I decree and declare that you have girded me with strength to battle: them that rise up against me hast thou subdued under me" (2 Samuel 22:40). I decree and declare that I am a soldier of the Lord. I surrender all to you, my mind, body, spirit, and soul. I realize that Satan desires to sift me as wheat (Luke 22:31) and that the devil is like a roaring lion, seeking who he desires (1 Peter 5:8). Father, I realize that you use my praise and worship, my singing, my praise dancing, and my calling as a weapon against the enemy. I will spread your word through preaching and teaching, song, dance, and service to you so that those whose minds have been blinded by the enemy (2 Corinthians 4:3-4) will be set free and delivered from the strongholds that have them bound. In the name of Jesus, I pray. Amen

We Are Soldiers

1. My mother was a Soldier, Oh yes! She had her hand on the Gospel plow, Oh Yes! But one day she got old, she couldn't fight anymore, she said I'll stand here and fight anyhow.

Woe oe.
Chorus:
"We are Soldiers in the army, we have to fight, although we have to cry; we have to hold up the blood-stained banner. We have to hold it up until we die!"

2. My father was a Soldier, Oh yes! He had his hands on the Gospel plow, oh yes! One day he got old, he couldn't fight anymore, he said I'll stand here and fight anyhow.

Oo- O - O!

Chorus:
"We are Soldiers in the army, we have to fight, although we have to cry; we have to hold up the blood-stained banner. We have to hold it up until we die!"

3. I'm so glad I'm a Soldier, Oh yes! I've got my hand on the Gospel plow, oh yes! One day I'll get old, and can't fight anymore, and I'll stand here and fight anyhow

Oo- O - O!

Chorus:
"We are Soldiers in the army, we have to fight, although we have to cry; we have to hold up the blood-stained banner. We have to hold it up until we die!"

Text: Gospel Hymn
Tune: Gospel Hymn arr. by Nolan Williams Jr., b 1969, @ 2000, GIA Publication Inc

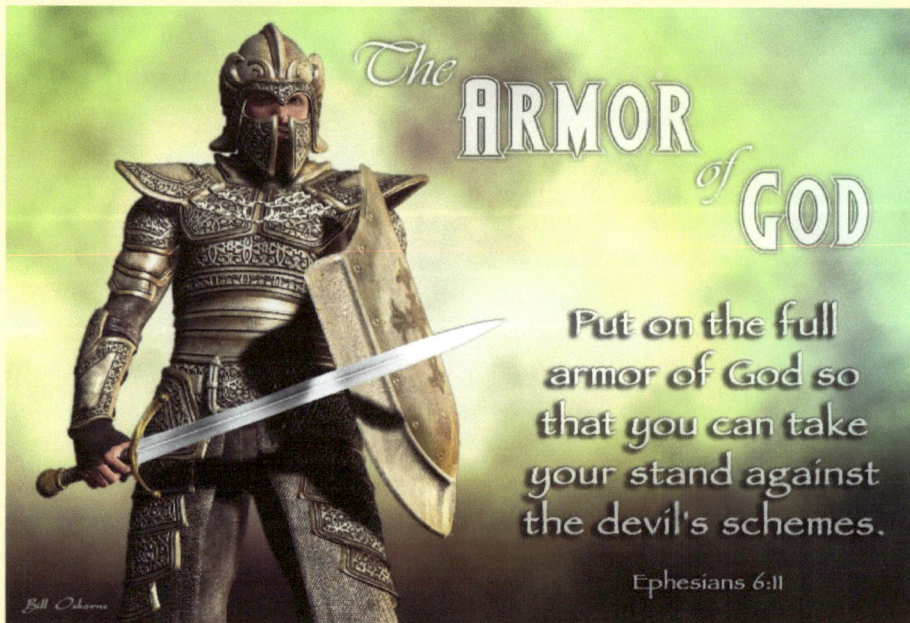

The ARMOR of GOD

Put on the full armor of God so that you can take your stand against the devil's schemes.

Ephesians 6:11

Day 1
Put on your Armor

"Wherefore take unto you the whole armor of God, that ye may be able to withstand in the evil day, and having done all, to stand." Ephesians 6:13

When the Roman army went out to war, they wore their armor. What is true in the natural is true in the spiritual. As soldiers in the Army of the Lord, we must put on the whole armor of God daily, so we can fight the enemy. We must withstand the day of evil by obeying God and his Word and preparing ourselves.

Types of Armor

1. **Defensive armor** or that which protected themselves: HELMET, GIRDLE, BREAST-PLATE, GREAVES or brazen boots, GAUNTLETS (a kind of gloves that served to defend the hands, and the arm up to the elbow) and the SHEILD (the gerron, the Pelta and the scutum)

2. **Offensive armor** or that by which they injured their enemies: SPEAR, LANCE, SWORD, AXE, IRON CLUB or MACE, the BOW, and the SLING.

Commentary on the Bible, by Adam Clarke, [1831], at sacred-texts.com

1 Timothy 6:11-14 (NLT)
[11] But you, Timothy, are a man of God; so, run from all these evil things. Pursue righteousness and a godly life, along with faith, love, perseverance, and gentleness. [12] Fight the good fight for the true faith. Hold tightly to the eternal life to which God has called you, which you have confessed so well before many witnesses. [13] And I charge you before God, who gives life to all, and before Christ Jesus, who gave a good testimony before Pontius Pilate, [14] that you obey this command without wavering. Then no one can find fault with you from now until our Lord Jesus Christ comes again.

We must pursue after the things of God: Righteousness, godly life, faith, love, perseverance, and gentleness and not the things of this world.

2 Timothy 2:3-4 (NLT)
"[3] Endure suffering along with me, as a good soldier of Christ Jesus. [4] Soldiers don't get tied up in the affairs of civilian life, for then they cannot please the officer who enlisted them."

Jesus Christ suffered pain so that mankind may be saved and delivered from sin, guilt, and shame. As strong soldiers in the Army of the Lord, we too must endure suffering for the cause of Jesus Christ. We must focus on the plan of God and not the things of this world.

Heavenly Father, *I am a soldier in your army and I will put on the whole armor of God daily to withstand the attacks of the enemy. I understand that I live in the world but I'm not of this world so I will not be tied up with the affairs of this world. I pursue righteousness, godly life, faith, love, perseverance, and gentleness. I must fight the good fight of faith in prayer and spiritual warfare. I decree and declare,* If God *be* for us who *can be* against us? (Roman 8:31); I decree and declare that God spared not his own Son, but delivered him up for us all (Romans 8:32A): I decree and declare that nothing will separate me from the love of Christ, no tribulation, or distress, or persecution, or famine, or nakedness, or peril, or sword? (Romans 8:35); I decree and declare that we are more than conquerors through him that loved us and I am persuaded, that neither death, nor life, nor angels, nor principalities, nor powers, nor things present, nor things to come, nor height, nor depth, nor any other creature, shall be able to separate us from the love of God, which is in Christ Jesus our Lord. *In Jesus name, I pray. Amen*

Prayer Journal

_____
_____
_____
_____
_____
_____
_____
_____
_____

Prayer Requests for Others and Myself

1. _____

2. _____

3. _____

4. _____

5. _____

6. _____

7. _____

8. _____

Day 2
Truth and Righteousness

Stand therefore, having your loins girt about with truth, and having on the breastplate of righteousness. Ephesians 6:14

Loins – are the sides between the lower <u>ribs</u> and <u>pelvis</u>, and the lower part of the <u>back</u>; reproductive organs (Preacher's Outline and Sermon Bible - Commentary - The Preacher's Outline & Sermon Bible – Ephesians).

Girded – to encircle with a belt or band; to fasten or secure; to equip or endow; to prepare

(oneself) for action (Preacher's Outline and Sermon Bible - Commentary - Ephesians).

The Belt of Truth - was used to hold the soldier's clothing next to his body and to strengthen and support the body" (Preacher's Outline and Sermon Bible - Commentary – Ephesians).

1. **Girded with truth** – we must be committed to reading, mediating, speaking, and praying the Word of God so when the enemy comes against you, your family, and the world we can use the Word of God to destroy the enemy.

When we are in Christ we become new creatures and our lives change for others (John 1:14, John 14:6). God will set us apart or declare us holy (John 17:17, Ephesians 5:26). We will begin to talk different and live our lives that are pleasing to the Lord (Ephesians 4:25; 1 Peter 1:22, Zechariah 8:16; Malachi 2:6).

2. The Word of God keeps us from being tossed back and forth by every attack of the enemy (Ephesians 4:14) and every battle and trial we will face (Hebrews 2:17-18; Hebrews 4:15-16) We must teach our families, love ones and even strangers the importance of the Word of God against the enemy.

The Breastplate of Righteousness - The breastplate covered the body of the soldier from the neck to the thighs. It was needed to protect the heart especially of the soldier so it does not be wounded" by the things, of this world and the enemy (Preacher's Outline and Sermon Bible - Commentary – Ephesians). We should seek the Lord with our whole heart and allow God to clothe us with his righteousness. When a man, woman, boy or girl is saved, God counts him or her righteous (Matthew 5:20, Romans 3:21-22, 1 Corinthians 15:34, 2 Corinthians 5:21, Philippians 1:11, Philippians 3:9 and Titus 2:11-12).

Father God, I want to thank you Lord for your truth and your righteousness. Lord, you are the way, the truth, and the life. Thank you for your grace. Thank you for being full of grace and truth. Sanctify and cleanse me with your word. Help me to speak truth to myself and others, and to walk in peace and love with you, Lord and others." (Preacher's Outline and Sermon Bible - Commentary - The Preacher's Outline & Sermon Bible – Ephesians) Father God, I gird my loins with truth so you will keep me from being tossed to and fro by every attack of the enemy. Thank you for being a merciful and faithful High Priest who made reconciliation for my sins and is touched with the feeling of my infirmities. Thank you that I can come boldly to the throne of grace that I may obtain mercy and find grace to help me in time of need. I put on the breastplate of righteousness that protects my heart. Thank you for filling my heart with the fruit of righteousness and for allowing me to walk in grace that brings salvation. My desire is to live soberly, righteously, and godly. In Jesus name, I pray. Amen

Prayer Journal

_____
_____
_____
_____
_____
_____
_____
_____
_____

Prayer Requests for Others and Myself

1. _____

2. _____

3. _____

4. _____

5. _____

6. _____

7. _____

8. _____

Day 3
Peace

¹⁵ And your feet shod with the preparation of the gospel of peace;
Ephesians 6:15

The sandals of the gospel – the sandals were a sign of readiness—readiness to march and to do battle. The Roman soldiers wore military boots or sandals called caliga on their feet. They were heavy sandals with thick soles studded with hollow-headed hob-nails and they gripped the ground. These boots were strong, allowing the soldier to stand firmly and cross safely on most any terrain. They were comfortable enough to allow the soldier to march at least 20 miles.

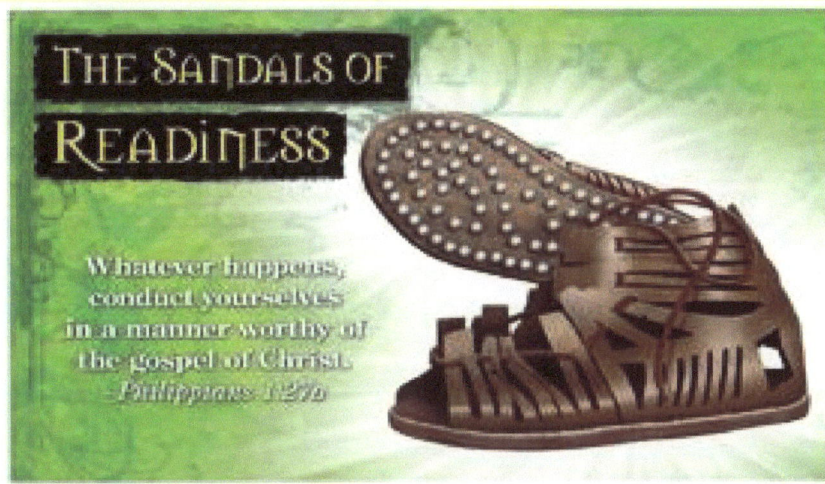

THE SANDALS OF READINESS

Whatever happens, conduct yourselves in a manner worthy of the gospel of Christ. -Philippians 1:27a

The sign of the good Christian soldier is that they are always ready to fight the good fight of faith and to spread the Word of truth wherever he or she goes, not matter what is happening or who one is with. As Christian soldiers, our lives should show others that we are children of God because of the love of God and the love shown for others.

Gospel of Peace – the peace we have with God through Jesus Christ.

We cannot "be ashamed of the gospel of Christ: for it is the power of God unto salvation to everyone that believeth; to the Jew first, and to the Greek" (Romans 1:16)

"But sanctify the Lord God in your hearts: and be ready always to give an answer to every man that asketh you a reason of the hope that is in you with meekness and fear" (1 Peter 3:15).

The spiritual footwear that comes from the "Gospel of Peace" gives us the firm-footed stability, promptness (on-time) and readiness ("be ye all so ready") to face the adversary, the devil and his imps, principalities, powers, rulers of the darkness and spiritual wickedness in high places. When we walk in the peace of God and spread the gospel of Jesus Christ, it counteracts the enemy's strategies.

Pastor Hayden of the Intercessors Conclave Ministry says, "When the child of God, one with a personal relationship with Him, goes into a confused place with their whole armor of God, it confuses the enemy." The atmosphere changes for the good because you are walking in the peace and power of God.

Don't let the enemy steal your peace you have found in Jesus Christ. We must speak the Word of God into the atmosphere wherever we go. Great peace comes from reading the Word of God.

Gracious Father
 I come in your presence with thanksgiving for the peace you have given me through Jesus Christ. I thank you for your Word, for it is the power of God unto salvation. I desire to have my feet shod with the preparation of the gospel of peace. I desire to be ready to march and bear witness of the gospel and be ready always to give an answer to every man, woman, boy or girl that asks me for the reason for the hope that is in me. The hope that is You. I need your peace right now. In Jesus Name, I pray. Amen

Prayer Journal

_____

_____

_____

_____

_____

_____

_____

_____

_____

_____

Prayer Requests for Others and Myself

1. _____

2. _____

3. _____

4. _____

5. _____

6. _____

7. _____

8. _____

Day 4
Shield of Faith

Above all, taking the shield of faith, wherewith ye shall be able to quench all the fiery darts of the wicked. Ephesians 6:16

The shield of faith in God.

"The word "shield" does not mean the small round shield which the soldier held in his hand to fight off the weapons of the enemy. It means the great oblong shield worn by the soldier to protect his body from the fiery darts thrown by the enemy."
(Preacher's Outline and Sermon Bible -Commentary – Galatians-Colossians)

"The Roman shield of the time was called a *scutum*. This type of shield was as large as a door and would cover the warrior entirely. Such a shield was not just defensive but could also be used to push warriors away" (www.gotquestions.org/shield of faith).

The enemy loves to attack the mind, bringing doubt and evil thoughts. Such fiery darts often assault the mind—one doubting and evil thought after the other—fighting against the will—struggling to get hold of the mind and subject it to doubt or evil. The Christian soldier is one who puts on the shield of faith, which is faith in God and lets God fight his or her battles.

Faith in God is a complete and perfect trust that God will quench and conquer the fiery darts of doubt and evil that attacks him or her.

We must receive Jesus as our personal Savior and reaffirm our faith in God every day as often as we can. Pray the shield of faith over yourself, family, friends, enemies, the world. and your family: We must read and mediate on the Word daily and rebuke the enemy and ask God to strengthen us daily.

Heavenly Father, I know that without faith it is impossible to please you so I will diligently seek you. I will study your word and communicate with you through prayer daily so my mind will stay on you. You are my strength and your grace is sufficient for me. I have faith in you because you are the lifter of my head. God, you are my help and shield. I am committing all my ways to you and thank you for directing my path. Father, God there are some areas of concerns that I need your help with. Please Lord help me to overcome (list areas of concerns) _____ I will carry my shield of faith daily so I can destroy the fiery darts of the enemy for others and myself In Jesus Name I pray, Amen.

Prayer Journal

_____

_____

_____

_____

_____

_____

_____

_____

_____

_____

Prayer Requests for Others and Myself

1. _____

2. _____

3. _____

4. _____

5. _____

6. _____

7. _____

8. _____

Day 5
Salvation and the Word of God

"And take the helmet of salvation, and the sword of the Spirit, which is the word of God:"
Ephesians 6:17

The Helmet of Salvation.

"The helmet covered the head and the mind of the soldier. The head, of course, was the core of a soldier's power to wage war. He or she must be able to discern and think on their feet and determine strategies with their thinking abilities. This was the most important factor in determining his or her victory or defeat. Therefore, the soldier needed a helmet to protect their head and mind. The sign of the Christian soldier is the helmet of salvation (deliverance). They must protect their mind and thoughts, keeping all thoughts focused on Jesus Christ. The helmet that protects the mind of the Christian soldier is *salvation*. Unless a man or woman has been saved, his or her mind cannot be protected from the fiery darts of temptation "(Preacher's Outline and Sermon Bible - Commentary - The Preacher's Outline & Sermon Bible – Ephesians).

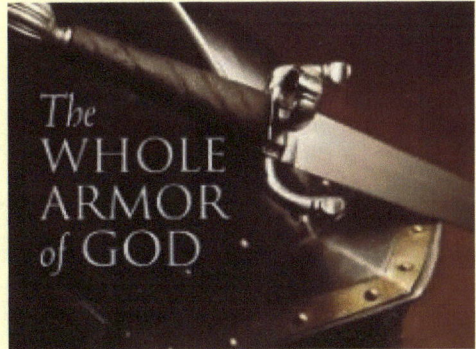

When we become saved we need to surrender our mind, body, spirit, and soul to God and let him renew our minds so we can do the work the Lord has called us to do. We will become new creatures and we will talk, look, see, hear, and think differently (Ephesians 4:22-24; 2 Corinthians 5:17).

If God called you to be an intercessor, prayer warrior, gatekeeper, and watchman we need to do it intercede for others as God intercedes for us.

"And he saw that there was no intercessor: therefore, his arm brought salvation unto him; and his righteousness, it sustained him. For he put on righteousness as a breastplate, and a helmet of salvation upon his head" (Isaiah 59:16-17).

The Sword of the Spirit is the Word of God. The sword was used both to protect and to fight off and destroy the enemy. The sign of a good Christian soldier is their knowledge of the Word of God. By using the Word of God, the soldier will protect himself or herself from the attacks of the enemy; and he/she fights and wins battle after battle, day after day. The Word of God is the one weapon that can ensure victory for the Christian soldier, for the "Word of God is living and active and sharper than any two-edged sword." We need to study God's Word and hide it in our hearts (Psalm 119:11)

Thank you Lord for the helmet of salvation that protects my mind from negatives thoughts. I decree and declare that I will think on things that are true, noble, right in your sight, pure, lovely, and admirable (Philippians 4:8 NIV). I surrender my mind body, spirit, and soul to you so you could get rid of my old deceitful desires and think like you think with a new attitude and clothed in true righteousness and holiness (Ephesians 4:22-24). Thank you for the Sword of the Spirit which is the Word of God. I decree and declare that I will carry your Word in my heart. I understand that I am not of this world so I will not be conformed to their ways but be transformed by the renewing of my mind, that I may prove what is that good, and acceptable, and perfect, will of God" (Romans 12:2). In Jesus Name, I prayer Amen.

Prayer Journal

_____
_____
_____
_____
_____
_____
_____
_____
_____
_____

Prayer Requests for Others and Myself

1. _____

2. _____

3. _____

4. _____

5. _____

6. _____

7. _____

8. _____

Be Still, God Will Fight Your Battles

Be still, God will fight your battles. Be still, God will fight your battles.
Be still, God will fight your battles. God will fight your battles
if you just keep still.

Keep a praying', God will fight your battles. Keep a prayin', God will fight your battles. Keep a
prayin', God will fight your battles. God will fight your battles
if you just keep still.

Keep a waitin', God will fight your battles. Keep a waitin', God will fight your battles. Keep a
waitin', God will fight your battles. God will fight your battles
if you just keep still.

Keep a singin', God will fight your battles. Keep a singin', God will fight your battles. Keep a
singin', God will fight your battles. God will fight your battles
if you just keep still.

I'm a witness, God will fight your battles. I'm a witness, God will fight your battles. I'm a witness,
God will fight your battles. God will fight your battles
if you just keep still.

African American Heritage Hymnal, 2001

Exodus 14:13-15

13 But Moses said to the people, "Do not fear! Stand by and see the salvation of the LORD which He will accomplish for you today; for the Egyptians whom you have seen today, you will never see them again forever. 14 "The LORD will fight for you while you keep silent." 15 Then the LORD said to Moses, "Why are you crying out to Me? Tell the sons of Israel to go forward.

LET GOD FIGHT FOR YOU

STAND STILL & SEE THE SALVATION OF THE LORD

EXODUS 14:13

Day 6
Keep on Praying

"Praying always with all prayer and supplication in the Spirit, and watching thereunto with all perseverance and supplication for all saints;"
Ephesians 6:18

Prayer is the Christian soldier's secret weapon so we should walk in constant prayer. We must be willing to pray at anytime, anywhere, with anyone. We must pray before we put on our armor, as we are putting on each piece of armor and after we put on our armor. The only way to fight the enemy is through prayer.

Communication is a vital element in any successful relationship, including our relationship with God. God wants us to communicate with Him about all our cares, concerns and even our joys. The best way to communication with God is through prayer. Prayer is much more than words. It is an expression of the heart towards God. It is an experience, a relationship – not an activity. Whatever we do we should start with prayer and end with prayer.

According to Preacher's Outline and Sermon Bible - Commentary – Ephesians, "Prayer is in the form of supplication for ourselves, and in the form of intercession for others - We must pray with all the parts of prayer; confession of sin, petition for mercy, and thanksgiving for favor received. And we must do it by the grace of God the Holy Spirit, in dependence of the Holy Spirit"

We must watch and pray (Matthew 26:38, Matthew 26:41, 1 Peter 4:7) with all perseverance – and never becoming discouraged and disheartened (Luke 18:1). We should not be weary in well doing: for in due season we shall reap, if we faint not (Galatians 6:9-10).

No matter how old or young you are, what title you have, what call you have on your life, prayer makes a difference. Along with the presence of the Lord, the atmosphere will change for the good, and the enemy will have to flee.

God is calling all of us into a relationship with Him.

Father God, I seek you, your strength, and your face continually (1 Chronicles 16:11). Thank you for praying for me and having me on your mind. You say in your word that I should ask, and it shall be given to me; seek, and I shall find; knock, and the door shall be opened unto me (Matthew 7:7). I will be careful about nothing; but in everything by prayer and supplication with thanksgiving let my requests be made known to God (Philippians 4:6). I will continue to pray for others. I will continue to watch and pray with all perseverance and supplication for all people (Ephesians 6:18).

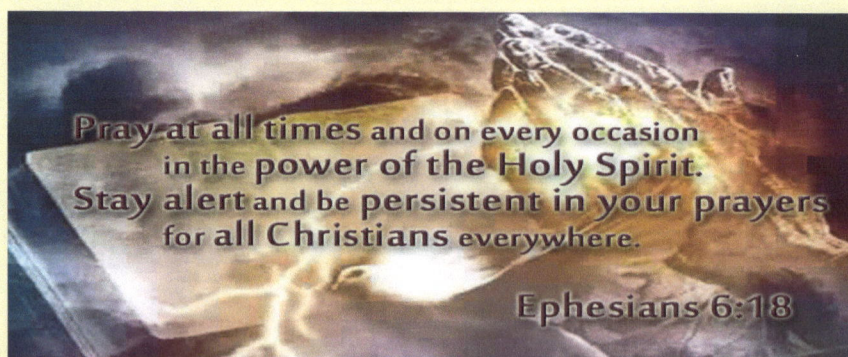

Pray at all times and on every occasion in the power of the Holy Spirit. Stay alert and be persistent in your prayers for all Christians everywhere.

Ephesians 6:18

Prayer Journal

_____
_____
_____
_____
_____
_____
_____
_____
_____

Prayer Requests for Others and Myself

1. _____

2. _____

3. _____

4. _____

5. _____

6. _____

7. _____

8. _____

Day 7
This Means War

When our enemies heard that we were aware of their plot and that God had frustrated it, we all returned to the wall, each to our own work.[16] From that day on, half of my men did the work, while the other half were equipped with spears, shields, bows and armor. The officers posted themselves behind all the people of Judah [17] who were building the wall. Those who carried materials did their work with one hand and held a weapon in the other, [18] and each of the builders wore his sword at his side as he worked. But the man who sounded the trumpet stayed with me.[19] Then I said to the nobles, the officials, and the rest of the people, "The work is extensive and spread out, and we are widely separated from each other along the wall. [20] Wherever you hear the trumpet, join us there. Our God will fight for us!" Nehemiah 4:15-20 (NIV)

Read Nehemiah 4:11-23

We are living in a time where the enemy is trying to deceive us and he wants to slowly destroy us; he knows his time is almost over. We must understand that people in other nations are experiencing economic depression, famine, oppression, and persecution because some of them have not accepted the Lord Jesus Christ as their Savior and some are just giving up on God. People are dying daily and God is calling us to intercede for those that do not know him and those that have given up on life.

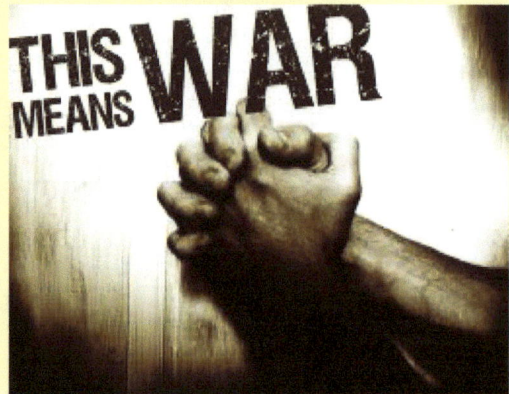

Nehemiah, the cup-bearer for the Persian king, King Artaxerxes in Susa was concerned about his Jewish brothers and sisters who had returned to Jerusalem from their exile and the wall in the temple was destroyed. Nehemiah decided to fast and pray on the behalf of the Israelites. Nehemiah had a burden on his heart to rebuild the wall with the help of his brothers. Nehemiah began to rebuild the wall.

According to Preacher's Outline and Sermon Bible KJV- Nehemiah, the rebuilt walls of Jerusalem, the Holy City represented

1. Security, protection from the enemies.
2. Spiritual separation
3. Deliverance and salvation.
4. The need for watchfulness and diligent gatekeeper, watchmen, doorkeepers, intercessors that will watch and pray. They needed a constant guard to stand watch against any attacks by the enemy. Spiritually, the believer must be vigilant in guarding him or herself.
5. God's presence, righteousness, provision, guidance, and blessings.

We must rebuild the walls of our churches. The enemy, Sanballat, the Samaritan governor, during Nehemiah's time and the devil during our time does not want us to rebuild the wall.

There are 4 strategies the enemy uses against us (Preacher's Outline and Sermon Bible KJV-Nehemiah)

1. The first strategy used by the enemy is that of ridicule, insults, and mockery but we can counteract that with prayer and perseverance.
2. The second strategy used by the enemy is that of conspiring, plotting to attack standing watch, overcome this strategy by standing watch and praying.
3. The third strategy used by the enemy is discouragement and fatigue but we can draw strength from God.
4. The fourth strategy used by the enemy is fear, threats, intimidation but we can be armed by trusting God's power.

Nehemiah was confronted by people who did not want the wall to be rebuilt but Nehemiah did not let that stop him, the men with him were warriors; they did not fear man but feared God. They watched out for the enemy as they worked. It is time for us to get families back together through prayer. Strongholds need to be dealt with so people can be delivered. God is looking for warriors who are bold for Jesus. Who do not mind standing the trenches for others as intercessors.

The enemy does not want are lives rebuilt, but that's his problem not ours. We shall live and not die and declare the works of The Lord. (Psalm 118:17 KJV)

In order to conquer the enemy; to stand against the enemy's strategies; we must be strong in the Lord, draw strength from him and put on the armor the whole armor of God. We must stop fighting with one another and wage war with the devil through our obedience to God, through our praise and worship, through our singing, through our preaching and teaching, through our daily living. Let us put our trust in God, and let The Holy Spirit use us for His Glory. No weapon formed against us shall prosper. (Isiah 57:17) For we are more than conquerors. (Romans 8:37)

As believers in the Lord Jesus Christ, we must take a stand for Christ and His righteousness.
We bear witness to His saving grace and proclaim to the world the way of righteousness, that men and women must obey the commandments of God. As a result, many unbelievers in the world oppose us. In some cases, they even persecute us through ridicule, scorn, plots, and schemes. In addition, they attempt to strike fear in our hearts through threats and intimidation. The answer to such attacks by unbelievers is twofold: we must arm ourselves and we must trust God's power to deliver us through the attacks.

Father God, I come in your presence to say thank you for everything you have done in my life, is doing, and will do. I worship you with my whole heart. Thank you for the call you have placed on my life. I will continue to rebuild the wall, one hand serving you and the other on my weapon, the sword of the spirit. I will put on the full armor of God daily so I can fight against the enemy. I pray for discernment and the eagle eye anointing so I can see the enemy coming from a distance and I can destroy him before he destroys us. I will stand on the wall and watch and pray. Praying with all prayer and supplication in the Spirit of God and watching with all perseverance and supplication for all saints. This means war, the enemy cannot have my family, my increase, or my breakthrough. I plead the blood of Jesus Christ. In Jesus name, I pray. Amen

Prayer Journal

_____
_____
_____
_____
_____
_____
_____
_____
_____
_____

Prayer Requests for Others and Myself

1. _____

2. _____

3. _____

4. _____

5. _____

6. _____

7. _____

8. _____

Conclusion

"And that, knowing the time, that now it is high time to awake out of sleep: for now, is our salvation nearer than when we believed. The night is far spent, the day is at hand: let us therefore cast off the works of darkness, and let us put on the armour of light. Let us walk honestly, as in the day; not in rioting and drunkenness, not in chambering and wantonness (running wild), not in strife and envying. But put ye on the Lord Jesus Christ, and make not provision for the flesh, to fulfil the lusts thereof." Romans 13:11-14 (KJV)

According to Preacher's Outline and Sermon Bible-KJV-Romans "Too many believers are *slumbering* and paying no attention to what is going on in the world; too many are not watching; too many are not observing the signs of the time. Too many are *complacent and slothful*, lazily passing through life with *little commitment* to serving Christ. Too few are meeting the needs of the suffering and dying masses of the world. It is time "to awaken" out of sleep: time to wake up, to be aroused and stirred. It is time to get up and to move and act—*now*—before it is too late."

We must watch and pray. 1 Peter 5: 8 says
"Be sober, be vigilant; because your adversary the devil, as a roaring lion, walketh about, seeking whom he may devour:"

Be sober — Avoid drunkenness of your senses, and drunkenness in your souls; be not overcharged with the concerns of the world.

Be vigilant—Awake, and keep awake; be always watchful; never be off your guard; your enemies are alert, they are never off theirs. (Clarke, Adam. "Commentary on 1 Peter 5:8". "The Adam Clarke Commentary". http://www.studylight.org/commentaries/acc/1-peter-5.html. 1832)

Wake up! Stop sleeping! We need to ask God for discernment and wisdom. Wake and pray. Wake up and let's slay our enemies.

Satan tempts us in three ways: (Preacher's Outline and Sermon Bible-KJV-Romans)

1. The subtle serpent; to beguile our senses, pervert our judgment, and enchant our imagination.

2. As an angel of light; to deceive us with false views of spiritual things.

3. As a roaring lion; to bear us down, and destroy us by violent opposition, persecution, and death.

Pastor Hayden informs us "that the devil has released a legion (6000) of demons against the fivefold ministry and against each piece of our armor." We need to learn all we can about the enemy because he studies us every day and from your reactions to different situations, he can tell what gets you upset, angry, etc.

Matthew 18:20 says "For where two or three are gathered in my name, there am I in the midst." Yes, the two or three must agree with what God is saying about a situation. Each one cannot have their own opinion because God does not get the glory during mess or confusion. God is not the author of confusion but God will confuse confusion and destroy the works of the enemy.

ARE YOU READY: THIS MEANS WAR!

Prayer Journal

_____
_____
_____
_____
_____
_____
_____
_____
_____
_____
_____

Prayer Requests for Others and Myself

1. _____

2. _____

3. _____

4. _____

5. _____

6. _____

7. _____

8. _____

FAMILY PRAYER TIME

Family time in prayer and study of the Word of God is very important.

You should:
1. Start your day with prayer with the family;
2. Choose a day and time you will read the Bible together;
3. Recite scripture, and even talk about what you have read;
4. Pray together as a family.

INDIVIDUAL PRAYER TIME:

Find a place in your home/apartment that will be your War Room.

1. Read a Scripture passage or two.
2. Pray short prayers focusing on who God is.
3. Ask for specific things for people you know and don't know.
4. Ask for specific things for yourself.
5. Thank God for what He's done and going to do.

FAMILY PRAYER LINES:

If you have family members who live in different places around the world, you could get a free conference line and schedule a day and time during the week to have a family conference call. This will strengthen the family.

Go online to www.NoCostConference.com and set up an account **(it's Free)**

Praying in the Spirit. Declaring the word of God over the lives other and ourselves and watching God move.

Sources

Barnes' Notes on the New Testament. Author Albert Barnes Jul 26, 2003 Commentary on the Bible, Adam Clarke, [1831], at sacred-texts.com

Clarke, Adam. "Commentary on 1 Peter 5:8". "The Adam Clarke Commentary". http://www.studylight.org/commentaries/acc/1-peter-5.html. 1832

Gotquestions.org/Shield of Faith (Copyright 2002-2017)

Matthew Henry Concise Bible Commentary – Ephesians https://www.studylight.org/ ver. 2.0.17.05.19 (2001-2017)

WORD *search* a division of Lifeway Christian Resources Word search Bible (POSB) (2017)

Preacher's Outline and Sermon Bible - Commentary - The Preacher's Outline & Sermon Bible – 1 & 2 Corinthians.

Preacher's Outline and Sermon Bible - Commentary - The Preacher's Outline & Sermon Bible – Ezra, Nehemiah, Esther.

Preacher's Outline and Sermon Bible - Commentary - The Preacher's Outline & Sermon Bible – Galatians, Ephesians, Philippians, Colossians.

Preacher's Outline and Sermon Bible - Commentary - The Preacher's Outline & Sermon Bible – Romans

Barnes, Albert. "Commentary on 1 Peter 5:8". "Barnes' Notes on the New Testament". http://www.studylight.org/commentaries/bnb/1-peter-5.html. 1870.

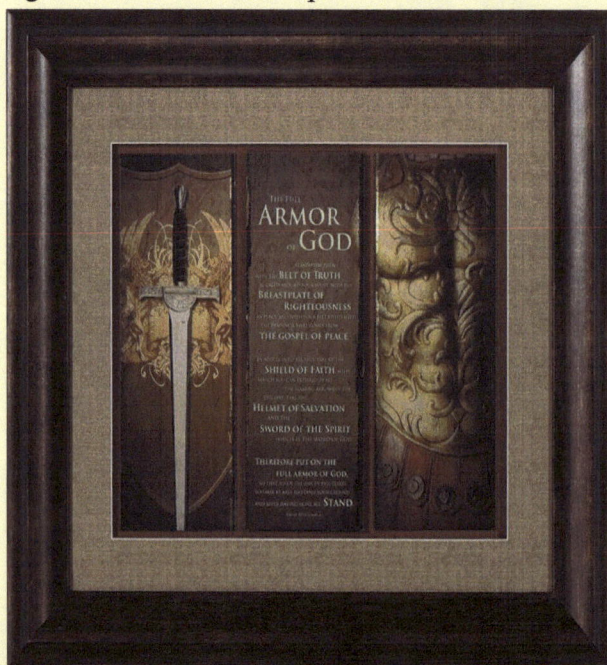

Reverend Sherrylyn Denise Womble, known to family and friends as 'Denise', is a native of New York City. She is the daughter of the late Eugene Daniels and Cynthia Womble-Brown and the eldest of three children. A product of the NYC public school system, her thirst for knowledge began at an early age. She always loved school and reading books which resulted in her being on the ARISTA honor roll for several years. The Lord has repeatedly proven Himself to be a way-maker in Rev. Womble's life. She was the first in her family to graduate from college, having obtained a Bachelor of Arts in majoring in Business Administration (with a Psychology/Law minor) from Baruch College. She graduated from Blanton Peale with a Certificate in Pastoral Counseling. She attained a Spiritual and Professional goal by concurrently completing her dual Masters Degrees in Divinity (M.Div) and Social Work (MSW) at NY Theological Seminary and Fordham School of Social Work. (respectively)

Being amongst the people of God is not new to Rev. Womble. She accepted Jesus Christ, at St. John's Baptist Church, at the age of 12. One Sunday morning, Sherrylyn says "the Lord lifted her out of the valley of dry bones the preacher took her hand and she gave Jesus her heart." She continued her walk attending Sunday school and served in the children and youth choir ministries. "How beautiful are the feet of them that preach the gospel of peace, and bring glad tidings of good things!" Romans 10:15.

Rev. Womble was licensed to proclaim the good news of Jesus Christ on November 27, 1994 and was ordained on November 14, 2010. She continues to serve faithfully as an associate minister and armor bearer to the Pastor of St. John's Baptist Church, Rev. John L. Scott. She is an extremely vital part of the St. John's Family. She serves as a member of the Board of Christian Education; The Superintendent of the Church School; The Prayer Ministry Coordinator; has graduated from the Evangelism Discipleship Training Program; works as a Christian Basic Training (CBT) and Board of Christian Education Instructor; is a member of the Missionary and Scholarship Ministries and one of the Facilitators of the Contextual Bible Study on Gender Based Violence.

She cherishes the Word of God is excited about the deep things of God and is a dedicated, compassionate prayer warrior interceding on behalf of those in need of deliverance and sacrificially ministers to the people of God. Faithfulness, humility, and Christ-like love characterize the gentle yet powerful spirit of this anointed woman of God. Rev. Womble is not ashamed to rejoice in the Spirit and 'bless the Lord at all times', recognizing that her victory lies in the praise. She knows that she is 'more than a conqueror' and that it was none other than the Lord who has blessed her with the precious gift of her son, Donnell Womble (graduated college), blessed her as a single parent, blessed her to complete college and strive toward the seminary, and has blessed her in ministry. Rev. Womble prays that The Lord will enlarge her territory through the vision God gave her in establishing and building SDW Healing Ministries and in expanding the ministry of the morning intercessory prayer and Bible Study group she facilitates "Sistah's of The Spirit and The Mighty Men of Valor" (S.O.S. & M.O.V.). Rev. Womble is a living example that God is a rewarder of them that diligently seek him. Hebrews 11:6
To God be the Glory

My Notes

www.ingramcontent.com/pod-product-compliance
Lightning Source LLC
Chambersburg PA
CBHW042012080426
42734CB00002B/57